I'm the BOSS.

*Reclaim Ownership of Your Life,
Build Your Dreams, and
Ditch Your 9-to-5*

Rachel Pedersen

Published by Author Academy Elite
P.O. Box 43
Powell, Ohio 43035
AuthorAdademyElite.com

Paperback ISBN: 978-1-64085-902-9

Library of Congress Control Number: 2019949349

I'm the BOSS.

*Reclaim Ownership of Your Life,
Build Your Dreams, and
Ditch Your 9-to-5*

CHAPTER 1

A dear friend of mine works in a job he absolutely hates. Every time I see him, it is an immediate topic of discussion. He rants, raves, and spews toxic details about his job, or rather, about the work environment that's poisoning his life.

As I look at my friend, I see the wear and tear his 9-to-5 has on his life—his eyes have bags underneath them. He's exhausted, never gets a good night's rest, works weekends and holidays, and often misses out on family get-togethers. "The man doesn't have my best interest in mind," he says, referring to his boss. "The man only has the bottom line in mind."

I see the happiness being sucked out of him daily. He's a fragment of the man I once knew, who used to be full of life and excited to start the day. I see a family who misses their brother, son, father, and grandfather holiday after holiday, and I see a body worn down and absent of vitality.

For months, I've encouraged him to leave, but relentlessly, he objects, "But I need job security," "I'm close to getting my pension," or even, "My health insurance benefits are unlike any other employer's." Though as I observe him, I see something different. I see a man whose dreams are on a shelf—waiting, begging, hoping he will remember them, clear the dust, and act.

He's undeniably and prematurely aging from the pressure, the stress, and the noise of his 9-to-5. In fact, in one of our recent conversations, his justification switched from determination, "I'm just seven years away from my pension," to apprehension, "If I keep working seven more years ... I wonder what will be left of me?" Unfortunately, his worrisome prediction is all too true.

You see, when we start our careers, we never say, "I will stay in this job for forty years, and I know it will be a dead end." We begin with excitement! But with each passing year, an overwhelming flood of jaded negativity drowns that excitement. We reassure ourselves we'll be healthy and active when it's time, "I'll stick it out until I can retire," or so we hope, "to golf, travel, and finally live the life I always dreamed of."

Wait a minute. We have.to stick it out—*for forty years!?*—in jobs we hate, working for bosses who would replace us in a heartbeat if we left or even worse, passed away? Yet, we delay really living our lives to the tail end … a time when life does not promise the happiness, health, or financial freedom we've been banking on those forty years.

So many of us wait to live out our dreams until the so-called *promise* of retirement, essentially allowing our bosses to dictate our entire lives, including the timeline on which we will finally chase our dreams. Now, that's a chilling realization.

When you accept a new job offer, you're not *only* accepting a paycheck and signing an NDA (non-disclosure agreement) or a non-compete, you're also signing away the rights to your vacation schedule, potentially your evenings and weekends, and perhaps even the rights to your own dreams. Jobs don't come with a "no strings attached" promise. Suddenly, we find ourselves tangled into countless strings. We end up putting on a show, going through the motions of the day with the master puppeteer controlling our every move.

You might know someone like my friend: someone who wakes up dreading work each morning, trudges through the day—eight, nine, or ten hours—only to come home exhausted. This someone has a family that instead of getting who they deserve, they get the leftovers. They're left with only a fragment of who their loved one is meant to be.

Often this life scenario plays out with one sipping ... no, drinking ... no, guzzling ... wine or other substances to numb the pressures and stresses of a 9-to-5. The 9-to-5, you don't even love, follows you home and continues to dictate your quality of life. The 9-to-5 that would easily replace you, now consumes you.

But wait. There's hope! Friday and the cheers of "TGIF, it's the weekend!" will come shortly enough. Yet, through the weekend, dread nags in the back of your mind saying, "This weekend only lasts for two days before I start the despised routine of Monday." Rinse and repeat for the next forty years, and then, my dear, you can finally enjoy your retirement.

I remember a story someone shared with me, her reflections about her life and biggest regrets. Day by day, she held onto her dreams—dreams of touring Greece, of visiting Italy, of family reunions ... all on hold until she retired. When she finally retired, she was met with the usual ailments of old age: aching knees, sore back, inability to travel, and ... her life was over. The window to capture her dreams and take advantage of the life she always wanted had closed. She gave her best years to a 9-to-5 which did NOT give her its best in return.

Completely unacceptable. We were made for better; we deserve better.

Imagine your child self sitting across from you. Looking up and watching you as you do nothing about your dreams, as you put them on a shelf to collect dust. What would your tiny self say to you today knowing how miserable you are? Those dusty dreams are familiar. I, too, have experienced this.

When I had my second child, Delilah, my 9-to-5 provided a mere four weeks of maternity leave. Four weeks! One month to spend bonding with my baby before returning to work. Then to give my baby to a nanny to raise, to bond with, cuddle, teach, educate, and inspire. My baby in someone else's arms, while I took care of my boss's babies—his business, legacy, family, as well as his retirement, golf, and vacation funds. Even though this was unacceptable to me, I didn't know differently. I didn't know another option existed. But in the back of my mind, something kept nudging me, "You are called to something greater."

At age sixteen, I dreamed of being a speaker, writer, influencer, thought leader. Now, what would my sixteen-year-old self say to the adult who reduced herself to a 9-to-5, who accepted a nominal paycheck in exchange for her dreams? What I didn't realize, and maybe you're not aware of this either, is that your paycheck is not money you're receiving every month. It's a deadly barter.

Imagine a conversation with *your* sixteen-year-old self, the one who had dreams before you knew how life would actually turn out. Imagine presenting your 9-to-5 checks as an offer to your teenage self—$2,000 every two weeks to hand over your dreams. Now, tell your aspiring teenager this: "You won't be able to travel the world, you won't be able to write that book, you won't be able to start that company that impacts millions of lives."

What will it take? $2,000 every two weeks? $50,000 a year plus benefits? Is that a fair trade? I can only imagine my own sixteen-year-old self looking at that offer and slapping it out of my adult self's hands. "How dare you put a price on my dreams!" that young lady would proclaim indignantly.

This is how seriously you need to take the attack from the 9-to-5, the 9-to-5 that's waging war on your dreams and the life you were called to live. It doesn't matter your age, salary, title, or accomplishments, you deserve to own and enjoy your dream life, a life on your own terms. *You deserve freedom.* Freedom—a word that means the power or right to act, speak, or think as one wants without hindrance or restraint.

That doesn't sound like your 9-to-5, does it? In fact, your 9-to-5 flies in the face of freedom.

To further illustrate, let's examine the antonyms of freedom because surely your 9-to-5 is not synonymous to freedom. Antonyms include impotence, inability, incompetence, responsibility, weakness, extreme, restraint, captivity, communism, confinement, difficulty, government, imprisonment, incarceration, limitation, reserve, restriction, servitude, slavery, subjection, subordination, and suppression. I don't know about you, but I don't want any of these words to describe my life nor the legacy I am meant to leave for this world.

Are those words creating an impending sense of doom or possibly a panic? "Rachel, how am I supposed to leave my 9-to-5?! How am I supposed to get out of this system? It's the only one I've ever known."

Today, I'm here to share with you that freedom is truly possible. I've done it myself, and I've helped thousands of people like you leave their 9-to-5 and embrace real, genuine freedom. So, please call me 'Captain Choo Choo' because today we're going on a journey. Hop aboard the Freedom Train Express! But first, I must warn you: Not everyone wants you to find freedom. Others will try to stop you. They will try to keep you miserable, stuck in your 9-to-5. They just don't understand the concepts I'm teaching you—concepts that reveal all that is possible, not only in this lifetime, but right away in the coming weeks if you choose to act.

Before we dive in, let's review who *not* to share your plans with. Your boss—regardless of how you feel about your boss or whether he or she is a good person, your boss's only desire in life is to keep you sitting down, shutting up, doing your job Monday through Friday, and thinking about your job Monday through Monday. This person will not be happy for you nor root you on during this journey; so, do not share it with them.

Your family—as unbelievable as this sounds, your family may not understand your journey toward freedom. I know, I know, it sucks, but many of your family members are still imprisoned in an antonym of freedom. They're trapped in their 9-to-5. They're miserable and brainwashed by the lies ingrained in our heads since we were kids in school.

You know one of the craziest things I've ever realized? School is nothing more than an indoctrination of a society teaching us to sit down, shut up, stand in line, not question orders, and work dutifully. Look at our society. One of my favorite times to observe is while commuting. While taking the light rail to work several years ago, I noticed a sea of machines surrounding me—people in suits, people with briefcases ... everyone looking miserable, reading the paper, reading a book, staring at their phones.

The mindless commute, the mindless commuters, the mindless 9-to-5ers, the mindless robots making their way to another day of making someone else's dreams come true while their own dreams rust.

As I looked around, I realized the brainwashing begins early. It's kind of scary if you think about it, but the purpose of school was actually to train the people, the population of the United States, to become good factory workers. I don't know about you, but I sure as heck don't aspire to become a factory worker, which, by the way, is a job that will be obsolete as the robots gradually take over ... Muahahaha.

CHAPTER 1 QUESTIONS FOR REFLECTION

1. What does happiness look like in my current situation? Will it last long-term?

_____

_____

_____

_____

_____

_____

_____

_____

_____

_____

_____

_____

_____

_____

_____

_____

_____

_____

_____

_____

_____

_____

_____

_____

2. What does freedom look like for me?

_____

_____

_____

_____

_____

_____

_____

_____

_____

_____

_____

_____

_____

_____

_____

_____

_____

_____

_____

_____

_____

_____

_____

_____

3. What possibilities are in front of me, waiting to be captured?

_____

_____

_____

_____

_____

_____

_____

_____

_____

_____

_____

_____

_____

_____

_____

_____

_____

_____

_____

_____

_____

_____

_____

_____

_____

_____

_____

CHAPTER 2

Once I realized the 9-to-5 was robbing me of my dreams, my decisions became easier. It was inevitable. The moment freedom entered my mind, I became obsessed, and within six short months, I left my 9-to-5. Today, I live a life, truly about freedom: financial freedom, freedom of time, and freedom of choice. I never ask a boss for vacation; I start as late as I want; I work as late as I want; I take weekends or weeks off; and I even work in places like the Dominican Republic, Spain, Mexico, and Puerto Rico.

The crazy thing you *need* to realize is this: you too can become "the boss." You can be the boss of your life. Once you understand that, once you get that transformative realization into your head, life will never look the same. Understand this: The rules about life and work are made up; the 9-to-5 is made up; the programming put into our heads as young kids was made up. And, here's the key: The things our parents told us growing up—you can be anything you want to be, you can do anything you want to do—are the actual truths about our lives. As you dive on in to this journey, in to perhaps the exact reason you purchased this book, I want you to embrace several mindset shifts.

First, don't be alarmed—naturally, your monkey brain will come out of nowhere, panicking, grasping for a sense of safety. It will side with all the inaccurate guidance you've received throughout your entire life. It's going to shout, "Don't leave your 9-to-5; that's your security! Just hang in there a bit longer … your pension is waiting! What will you do without health insurance?"

I saw a Facebook status one evening from a family friend—he mentioned that he had lost his secure corporate job. "Goodbye, I will miss you all," he signed off. He wasn't saying goodbye to his job; he was saying goodbye to the world. Suddenly the rug ... pulled out from beneath him. Twenty years of loyal service ... vanished in a day, along with it a pension he was counting on. Now obsolete. And, health insurance? Gone. Just like that.

This book will walk you through several steps beginning with reprogramming your mindset. You must believe you can become the boss of your life. To embrace the "boss mentality," we will walk through a couple exercises designed to give you freedom of mind and reverse the brainwashing you went through in school and perhaps in your current 9-to-5.

Our world is changing. Social Security may not be around forever. Health benefits aren't guaranteed. Your job is not as safe as the corporate brainwashers lead you to believe. No, the greatest security you can ever create for your life and your family is one that hinges on your own dreams and your own vision for your life.

Step 1: Reprogram. Are you ready to reprogram your mind? This will be intense, and yes, you will have days where you wonder, "Am I doing the right thing?" but there will also be days that will prove to you that the battle is worth it. Combatting the societal norm of succumbing to a 9-to-5 is worth it. The alternative is allowing your dreams to die a slow and toxic death. When I say "toxic," I've chosen this strong word for a reason. It's not toxic to have a dream, but to let a dream die inside of you is lethally toxic. First, it'll poison your mind—make you jaded, angry, upset, unfulfilled. And then, it'll manifest throughout your body (a lesson for a different day).

Step 2: Plan. We will create a plan of action stemming around the vision for your life. Pretend you don't have a job or a boss to report to every Monday. What will you do? Will you take your kids to the farmer's market? Will you go to that concert you've been dying to see? Maybe you will finally spend a week on the ocean, writing that book that's been inside of you forever? What will freedom allow you to do?

Step 3: Act. Your vision is the catalyst, and acting is absolutely essential, a NON-NEGOTIABLE. Sometimes people say, "Do you ever feel like one of those bums who doesn't have a job?" and the answer is "No!" Not because I'm defensive, but because I'm confident I work as hard if not harder than anyone I know, and it's toward something I absolutely love.

The biggest difference between a hobo (or mooch) who stays on people's couches and a dreamer is action. You must move, implement, ACT! Intention is nothing without action. Some say faith without work is dead. I believe a vision or a dream without action is a wish, a wish that can blow away in the wind. A wish means nothing and holds no weight. So, you *must* commit to taking your first step (then the next, and the next, etc.). Your future is yours. You deserve this.

CHAPTER 2 QUESTIONS FOR REFLECTION

1. Am I trusting/relying on entitlements (social security, pension, etc.) to sustain me through retirement?

_____

_____

_____

_____

_____

_____

_____

_____

_____

_____

_____

_____

_____

_____

_____

_____

_____

_____

_____

_____

_____

_____

_____

_____

2. What dreams do I currently have that are waiting to be experienced?

_____

_____

_____

_____

_____

_____

_____

_____

_____

_____

_____

_____

_____

_____

_____

_____

_____

_____

_____

_____

_____

_____

3. What dreams would the younger version of myself wish I
   were pursuing?

_____

_____

_____

_____

_____

_____

_____

_____

_____

_____

_____

_____

_____

_____

_____

_____

_____

_____

_____

_____

_____

_____

4. What action steps can I take TODAY and TOMORROW to make this happen?

_____

_____

_____

_____

_____

_____

_____

_____

_____

_____

_____

_____

_____

_____

_____

_____

_____

_____

_____

_____

_____

_____

_____

_____

_____

_____

CHAPTER 3

I'll never forget my first day of freedom after leaving my 9-to-5. I lazily laid in bed until 9:30 a.m. Previously, my alarm went off at 7 a.m. to get out the door on time even though I was always five minutes late to work.

Mornings have historically been my least favorite time. Stretching across the bed, I picked up my phone, checked my email, and realized I had no emergencies. I knew if I wanted to, I could literally sit in bed and watch TV shows while working for the day, but instead, I got up and began working on my business. It was one of the most surreal feelings I've ever had.

I didn't have to worry about going to the bathroom too many times and drawing the evil eye from Eleanor at the office. Before lunch, I had as many cups of espresso as I wanted without being away from my desk because when your office is your cell phone, you can literally work from anywhere. And lunch time? Oh my gosh, I went to Chipotle and ordered a huge burrito bowl and I took my sweet time eating every delicious bite of it … not rushing back, not feeling guilty if my lunch went long, not building someone else's business. In fact, I handled business from my phone *at* Chipotle. The feeling was absolutely dreamlike.

My husband called me from his day job and asked if I could pick up some diapers for our daughter. Without even thinking, I said, "I can't until 5:00," but then I suddenly realized, "Yes, I can," and so I did. Score! One less errand to check off that evening, which pre-freedom, robbed me of time with my family. That precious, precious time stolen for too many years from exhausted, overworked, and stressed-out me.

Incredible awareness hit me as I walked through Target and noticed the store was nearly empty, except for a couple of stay-at-home parents, a few retired folks, and some teenagers (likely skipping school). The magnitude of my freedom overwhelmed me! I broke down right there, realizing and celebrating that I would never arrive and depart as everyone else was. I could take my time, pull up to the front of the line, checkout, and not have to fight with everyone else who's stuck in a 9-to-5.

Imagine this. The world was now my playground—Target, Chipotle, library, park—they were mine (and will be yours, too). I was experiencing life in a way that very few can achieve, unless they are stay-at-home parents, retired grandparents, or school-skipping teenagers.

Another moment I will never forget: I went to San Francisco to speak at an event and as I booked my tickets and my hotel room, I became aware of my personal and professional power—no need to request approval for vacation time, and no need to ask someone else if it was convenient for them. The only question I had was, "Do you have Wi-FI?" But then, an intense nagging feeling came over me. You see, my husband was still in his 9-to-5. Every day I woke up to my playground and felt guilty he was still in chains. Everyone deserves freedom. I set myself on a massive journey to scale my business, chase bigger dreams, and ultimately free my husband, but that's not what this chapter is about.

This chapter is about *you*.

Deep down, you might feel undeserving of freedom. It's a self-punishing mechanism, like you don't deserve to be happy, to go after your dreams. Maybe somewhere along the way, a boss, a mentor, or maybe even a family member lead you to believe you weren't deserving of phenomenal things. The reality is—you deserve freedom. Yes, *you*, exactly as you are. You, today. You, now! You deserve freedom, and I want to help you get that into your head.

You must understand, entrepreneurs don't have some common denominator, nor were they selected to be part of some supernatural group of people lucky enough or deserving enough to leave the confines of the 9-to-5. No. The reality? They were lucky enough to hear that freedom existed. They got it in their head before it was too late. And then, they simply worked for it.

A gift awaits you ... the gift of freedom, and all you have to do is accept it. The ridiculous part is that we, as humans by nature, assume a law of reciprocity also awaits us. We believe that if something is given to us, strings are attached. Or, that in order for us to receive something, we must have done something worthy. Not true! Freedom is a "no strings attached" gift that you give yourself, family, friends, and future generations to come. The most difficult part of this entire process? You must step forward and decisively say, "I accept this gift."

If you don't, your gift remains unclaimed. Your dreams remain unclaimed ... along with that vacation you've always wanted to take with your family, along with your goals of leisure golf, giving back, and along with having the financial ability to help so many more people than you could in your 9-to-5.

Perhaps it's just my midwestern upbringing. After all, I'm just a mom from Minnesota. Remember, it was programmed into our minds somewhere along the way, or multiple points along the way. As young students, we became indoctrinated in the 9-to-5 plan or school of thought, and we began believing that if we didn't fall in line, we were rebels, the crazy ones. To an extent, that's true, but you don't have to follow "the plan" prescribed to you based on your ACT or SAT score.

Just as I shared that initially I felt uncertain—at times I even forgot I was free—you, too, will experience some weird feelings. Perhaps it's guilt. Maybe it's a feeling like you owe your boss something, or maybe you don't want to leave your spouse stuck in a 9-to-5. I get it. I've been there.

Let me illustrate: When an airplane encounters danger, the flight attendants direct you to put the oxygen mask on yourself before you help anyone else. The exact same concept is 1000% true for you and freedom. As much as you want to help your spouse, sister, boss, or coworkers find freedom, you must first claim your own. When you understand how deserving you are of this gift—the gift of freedom—you will then and only then be able to help others discover the same.

During my first two years as an entrepreneur—I have to be honest—some family and friends didn't understand my work. Sometimes the questions were almost silly, "When do you have free time to meet for lunch?" When I explained that I created my own schedule, the looks would almost instantly turn into a look of skepticism. "Yeah, sure, but when does your work allow it?" Others aren't used to managing their own schedules, but the cool thing is, as you find your own path out of this crazy world of 9-to-5 and false security, a day will come when others will ask how they can do the same. Do you see now why it is so essential that you grasp this idea of freedom and why you deserve it exactly as you are?

I have a good friend who, despite trying multiple diets and exercise routines every single year, finds himself in the same spiral. He'll lose a couple pounds and then unintentionally self-sabotage. Maybe it's just a weekend away or perhaps it's the holidays, but before he knows it, he weighs exactly the same as he did before. A part of his mind can't identify with being fit, healthy, and confident. Self-sabotage invades his mind every time he pictures what he might look like healthy and fit, including how the world might perceive him. You will likely experience this form of self-sabotage and self-limiting beliefs as go on your journey, too.

If you find yourself saying, "Who am I?" and, "What have I done to deserve freedom and happiness?" you're not alone.

We must first retrain our thoughts to initiate a cycle of positivity. In fact, I created a mantra for you: "I deserve freedom and the happiness that comes from it." Say this to yourself every single day. The power of the words that you speak in your life are either damning or life-giving.

Your brain is one of the greatest machines you will ever own and operate. It's continually learning, and based on the programming that you give it, it either creates and enforces neural pathways or it shuts them down and makes it impossible for them to exist. If doubt or even a shred of fear exists in your head, it is suggesting, "I am not worthy of happiness and freedom." Your new mantra will oppose it and bring life. As you say the words to yourself every day, you will discover that your happiness and freedom has been inside of you waiting to be released.

Make a list of everything you've heard throughout your lifetime that makes you believe a 9-to-5 is the most secure option and only option you deserve. Take a moment to review these common beliefs:

- Your 9-to-5 is the only guaranteed paycheck you'll ever get.
- Ninety percent of small businesses fail.
- Entrepreneurship is only for Silicon Valley.
- You can't create your own business when you have a family that depends on you.
- Health insurance is too expensive.
- You'll never have a retirement plan.
- School is the only way to get ahead.
- Your only chance at making more money is through working your way towards a promotion.

Can you see the emerging patterns? It's alarming, but you've probably heard these and many other myths. Embrace the idea now that you will be happy, fulfilled, successful, and rich. You *deserve* to be happy, fulfilled, successful, and rich. Each of those traits point to one thing. You have a gift, waiting to be opened—your freedom and the happiness that comes along with it.

CHAPTER 3 QUESTIONS FOR REFLECTION

1. Where can I see myself enjoying my freedom?

_____

_____

_____

_____

_____

_____

_____

_____

_____

_____

_____

_____

_____

_____

_____

_____

_____

_____

_____

_____

_____

_____

_____

_____

2. What possibilities most excite me?

_____

_____

_____

_____

_____

_____

_____

_____

_____

_____

_____

_____

_____

_____

_____

_____

_____

_____

_____

_____

_____

_____

_____

3. Who/what do I look forward to meeting for lunch/dinner/
brunch/mimosas?

CHAPTER 4

What if I told you your 9-to-5 is training you to believe your skills, values, and dreams are worthless? I know it sounds super dramatic, but from the moment you start your 9-to-5, your ability to perform is reduced to little more than a résumé. Kinda crazy if you think about it. Your significance is so much more than two pages of Times New Roman size 14 font could ever, ever explain. Yet, at some point, you started believing that pieces of paper, such as a degree, résumé, or cover letter were enough to define your very existence and worth. I don't blame you. It's not your fault.

The corporate system trains you to believe this. They don't want you to discover your value and what you're capable of unlocking. That could prove catastrophic for corporate positions. Imagine what they would have to pay you if you were able to demonstrate your skill and value to the world. Your dreams, skills, and passions are much more than a simple degree, résumé, or cover letter.

Think about it this way (while putting it into your context). You bring wonderful ideas to team meetings, you are creative, and maybe you have a plan for how the company might improve. Possibly you have an innovative solution that will change the trajectory of the company, only to be shot down with fear of failure as the board votes you down, again.

How many times have you worked effortlessly, tirelessly on a job, or maybe it was on a particular project—spending hours, days, maybe even weeks or months—where you poured your heart into it, but at the next meeting with the boss, you learn that they've scratched the project. All your work is completely invalidated. What's worse? This may lead to small breakdowns of how you perceive your value.

It is for this reason you must understand that you are more than a corporate cog. You've been led to believe your ideas were only valuable if, and only if, the entire board voted to approve them in the weekly—boring as heck—meeting. You know exactly what I'm talking about … those never-ending meetings with no purpose, only to puncture your ideas, not with bullets, but something even more dangerous: doubt. It only takes a couple of minutes for your passion-filled ideas to be destroyed and abandoned on a boardroom table. You need to recognize this pattern in your own corporate workplace.

Think about the countless "good ideas" that kept moving forward despite unfriendly fire. Even with resistance to their ideas, some of the best inventors in the world—Walt Disney, J.K. Rowling, Oprah Winfrey, and many more—are revered for their passion and innovation. Their ideas are still alive and well today!

Boardrooms with people, whose imaginations had rusted, rejected each of these innovator's proposals. If these world changers had listened to the criticisms, they would have abandoned the projects for which they eventually became known. But thankfully, some stroke of genius, and maybe a little bit of "crazy," allowed these trailblazers to pursue their passions and dreams.

The thought of a world without their inventions is terrifying. They inspired hundreds of thousands, and possibly millions of dreamers to never give up, and you, yes YOU, are no different. The moment you seize the veto power from the boardroom and say, "This is my dream and I'm standing by it," is the moment you join the ranks of the greats who defied convention, challenged the corporate cog status, and decided to stand for something greater. Every one of those inventors deserves a t-shirt that says, "I'm the Boss," because somewhere along the way, they dared greatly enough to turn from the boardroom and embrace their dreams. Yes, it's a profound act of defiance.

Just to be clear, I am **NOT** suggesting that next Monday you waltz in and declare you're leaving and pursuing your dream … unless, of course, you have the reserves and the ability to do so. I would have left sooner if it weren't for my responsibilities. Please hear me when I say I'm not advising you to immediately burn your boats and desert your 9-to-5. That would be crazy, and I'm not about *too* much crazy. Although I do love a little crazy.

You are more than just a moving part in a corporate machine. What if instead you could be the entire machine, the brains operating the machine, or the inventor of the machine? Your first step is to understand how doubt works and how your employer is using it to keep you from claiming "the boss" status in your life. Yeah, it's kinda maddening, but they're actually using doubt to keep you confined. It makes it a lot easier to pay you $50,000 a year plus benefits, doesn't it? If they can instill doubt in your head—doubt about your dreams, your abilities, and your skills—then they are less likely lose you to the dreams you shelved. Today, I want you to declare, "<u>I am a dreamer, and one day soon, I will be</u> **<u>The Boss</u>**."

What are the first action steps to believing this? So many people who have successfully gone after their dreams and claimed "the boss" status talk about mindset, which is especially important for you. If you're like me, I wasn't raised in a household where dreams and entrepreneurship were the norm. I was raised to follow the rules our teachers gave us: find a 9-to-5, submit a résumé, sit down, shut up, don't stand out, and don't be the hero. After a lifetime of hearing that script over and over and over again, it programs your mind. Today begins your reprogramming, and it all starts with mindset.

Instead of revising your résumé for the umpteenth time, or repositioning your cover letter in the hopes of securing a better paying job, write out the truths about yourself. Maybe they're the truths that once were, or maybe they're the truths that are yet to be. Take fifteen minutes and write out truths about your skills, talents, passions, and dreams. I'll never forget the first time I did this, and the results, still to this day, send chills down my spine. I wrote down the truths of dreams I had held onto quietly for years. Thankfully for me, they hadn't collected too much dust. The longer your dreams have been sitting on the shelf, the harder this is going to be; so, be warned.

I captured my dreams on paper: I wanted to write a book; I wanted to make a million dollars in my business; I knew I had the skills to lead a room at live events; and, I knew I was good at speaking, sharing, and connecting with people. It became evident I was meant for the stage. I was meant to build something bigger than anything I had ever seen put together by the people in my world. Another truth is that my ideas are brilliant, and *that* one took me some time to embrace. Write down your truths and hold tight to them. Now that you understand your corporate 9-to-5 gig is trying to confine you, you surely get the importance of holding your dreams close and immersing your brain in the new reality that you too can be the boss.

Looking back at the truths I recorded just three short years ago, I get chills … Every single one has become my reality. What dream would send chills down your spine as it comes to life? What truth would you want everyone to recognize? Imagine people talking about you and your idea … what would you want them to say? If you're looking for affirmation inside a boardroom or 9-to-5 meetings, I hate to break it to you, but it won't happen. They don't see you for the wonderful, complex, dream-fulfilled, awe-inspiring person you are. Quite possibly the most transformational thing I've realized is—it's not me and it's not you, it's *them*.

Your truths and dreams, once written out, take on a life of their own. You will experience massive shifts in your world as you discover that *all of your dreams* are possible when you breathe life into them. Before you declare you're leaving your 9-to-5 forever, I want to set you up with some skills that will help you understand and navigate the world of being your own boss. I'm excited for you because this will affect other areas in your life as you remove self-doubt, gain confidence, and as you stop others from littering their doubts into your dreams. The opinions of others will no longer hold a candle to the light of truth you hold dear to yourself.

If at all possible, use some vacation time to soul search into your truths. What did your sixteen-year-old self dream of? What did you journal about when you were a kid? And, if you are reading that line saying, "Rachel, I don't have enough time off. My job only gives me two weeks," well then, you're in luck, because it's about time that you started to create a life that you don't need a vacation from, one that is on your own terms, all the time.

CHAPTER 4 QUESTIONS FOR REFLECTION

1. What former beliefs about security do I need to release?

_____

_____

_____

_____

_____

_____

_____

_____

_____

_____

_____

_____

_____

_____

_____

_____

_____

_____

_____

_____

_____

_____

_____

_____

_____

_____

2. What truths do I know?

_____

_____

_____

_____

_____

_____

_____

_____

_____

_____

_____

_____

_____

_____

_____

_____

_____

_____

_____

_____

_____

_____

_____

_____

3. By when do I anticipate leaving my 9-to-5?

CHAPTER 5

Prepare to be gut-punched. I'm willing to bet you've created a vacation Pinterest board listing all the places you want to go, things you want to see, and stamps you want to one day proudly display on your passport.

Now, compare that board to your current passport stamps. What percentage of your dream trips have you completed? Fifty percent? Twenty-five percent? Or, closer to one percent or less? If you're anything like me, your Pinterest board, with all of your dream trips and travels, has hundreds of beautiful locations you dream of seeing. Maybe some are in the United States, maybe that place in Costa Rica you've always wanted to hike, or perhaps you want to see the beautiful snow and ice of Greenland.

Now, ask yourself this serious question. Am I on track to achieve these trips before I retire or am I too old to travel the way I've always dreamed? This is a critical reflection because traveling is something we always say we will do "someday," but "someday" often never comes.

Staycations replace vacations—it's a vicious cycle. First, you use a day or two of PTO (Paid Time Off) when you're sick or your kids have events at school; then, you spend the last of your savings fund designated for travel to pay off that expensive medical bill; before you know it, family is coming into town and being present with them sucks up the last of your PTO.

Now, you no longer have a plan for travel, but a wish and a Pinterest board. You have dreams running through your head of visiting those beautiful places in the South

Pacific—you know, the ones with those cool little pod things on the water? These hopes have quickly withered and turned into budget stays at motels. Your two weeks PTO no longer becomes fourteen days of bliss-filled travel and vacation, but instead stolen time, soaked up by incidental illness, three-day weekends, or maybe even a family reunion in another state.

Don't get me wrong, we need all of those things in our lives, but my question to you is this: *When do you plan on fulfilling that Pinterest board bucket list of beautiful dream-filled travel?*

In case you haven't figured it out yet, two weeks PTO is NOT enough to live the life you've always wanted, traveling to multiple countries or maybe even provinces and states within your own country. It's not enough to finally visit that cousin who lives in New York. It's not enough to take your kids to see national landmarks and amazing historical places, even if they teach them more about history than a history class ever will.

Before I became the boss of my own life, my travel résumé was pathetic. I had been to five different states within the United States, didn't own a passport, and had no plans of traveling to exciting, dream-worthy places anytime soon. The moment I became the boss, something ironic happened. The travel opportunities I had always wanted came to me. When you live a life full of hope, excitement, and inspiration, magic happens. People become magnetized towards you, and before you know it, you receive countless invites to conferences, events, and sometimes even speaking gigs.

Throughout the first year I traveled to thirteen states! For me, this was exhilarating. I am living! Hopping on a plane is one of my favorite feelings in the world, and now I am actually experiencing it ... regularly. In my new way of life, I never have to ask a boss for approval to go on a vacation with my family, go to a conference, or to speak at an awesome event. When I retired my husband from his 9-to-5, suddenly we could work from anywhere resulting in amazing dream trips filled with incredible memories. The best part of all is we never had a denial of a request for vacation.

This is partly why I'm so obsessed with building a business that allows me to operate from anywhere. I experienced more travel the following year than I had in my lifetime! India, Mexico, Spain, Puerto Rico, the Dominican Republic … the list goes on and on. I easily stayed in touch with my business as long as we had a wi-fi signal, of course.

Suddenly, the transformation within my own head and my own ability to dream became life-changing. Think about the last time you were shopping for last-minute flights. This is something I occasionally do. I look for beautiful Airbnb houses and last-minute flights just to see if we can put together a random fun vacation or, as I like to call it, workcation.

As you look up those trips, whether through Airbnb or using Groupon, what keeps you from hitting the beautiful red "Book Now" button? If the answer is finances, hang tight, anything can change in a month's time. When you're the boss, you create your paycheck and your own lifestyle. More likely than not, what's keeping you from pushing the button is the sinking, sinking feeling of having to wait to travel until all the stars align—your boss approves your vacation, you have the money in your savings account, and your schedule aligns with your spouse's and boss' schedules as well. Geesh, this makes travel really hard, especially spontaneously. Forget that!

Last year, our best friends asked us to go to Disney World and work for the week from there. For a moment, I experienced PTSD—feeling of "I can't do that, I have to work!"—because remember, that is exactly what we've been programmed to believe. What happens when the rules change? You're the boss, and no one can tell you "no" to the trips you want to take and the experiences you want to share with loved ones. As I got over the initial aftershock, we said "yes," and spent a week working part of the day, enjoying Disney World, living it up at night, and simply creating amazing memories.

This isn't just about PTO. I want you to think about the last time you took a vacation that, of course, your boss approved. When you were on the trip, was there that little nagging voice in your head saying, "Oh my gosh, I will have so much work waiting for me when I get back." Did that anxiety make it difficult to sleep or wake up in the morning? Did it make it difficult knowing that every day that passed was one less day of vacation, and you'd have to wait nearly a year for the next one ... IF you were lucky?

When you're the boss, you're able to do as much or as little work as you want on any trip so you can decide whether or not it's a workcation. You can wake up and go to bed without the nagging anxiety that a pile of papers waits for you when you get back.

I never knew travel could bring so much happiness. This past year, we took our kids to Disney World, we went to Mount Rushmore in an RV, and we even worked from our family cabin. Previously, the family cabin was only for weekends, but today, as the boss, we can go Monday through Friday, Monday through Monday, or whatever arrangement we want. We even purchased a vehicle with a 4G Hotspot built in so a long trip wouldn't hinder my ability to work. Game changer! By the time we arrive at our dream destination, my work is finished, and I'm able to unplug and enjoy the trip. This is what it's all about. This. Is. Living.

Take a moment to consider the first alternative of the two alternatives, which is how most people live their lives. Year after year slips by with no travel or vacation. With each passing year, your Pinterest getaway dream board grows while your passport collects dust sitting on that shelf next to your dreams. Maybe there's an occasional trip every two to five years. Maybe you're saving your PTO for the end of your career which is incredibly risky.

We all know employers can and will replace us. You might think you're irreplaceable, but the economic shifts in the United States over the last decade prove that no one, **ABSOLUTELY NO ONE**, is untouchable. The moment they let you go, all that PTO and potential vacation time you spent years storing up, instantly incinerate. Oh, the regret! Why didn't I take my kids on that vacation? Why didn't I go to Jimmy's basketball game? Why, why, why? I can't live with you experiencing regret like this.

The other alternative is waiting until retirement to travel. Consider for a minute the retired people you know. Some are in good spirits and great health, right? Wonderful! That's awesome for them! Take an honest look at yourself. Do you take care of your body? Do you exercise? Are you drinking enough water? Or is the stress and frustration of suppressing your dreams wearing you down? The wearing down becomes exponentially more apparent as the years go on. Let's exclude those exceptional people who get to sixty-five and look like movie stars. Think about your grandparents or an aunt or uncle. Maybe they've been having a lot of joints replaced or later in life, they've become progressively sick. It's not that easy to just start traveling after decades of remaining still.

I mentioned earlier, a conversation that haunts me almost every day. It reminds me to book my dream trips sooner rather than later. When we chatted, the woman was eighty years old and shared her dreams of going to Greece. That was the plan! However, at sixty-five, she realized she waited too long—her body and finances couldn't support that dusty dream.

Let's talk about other regrets. The regrets of the dying fascinate me. It sounds morbid but is incredibly inspiring. Regrets of people in their final days leave a blueprint of the beautiful lives we need to live today, not tomorrow. A leading regret of the dying is working too much. Another is not spending enough time with their kids. It boils down to not fully living life.

You see, today is not promised, but what I can promise you is that two weeks PTO is not enough to live the life you have been dreaming about.

CHAPTER 5 QUESTIONS FOR REFLECTION

1. What are my top ten dream places to visit?

2. What do I envision doing while I'm there?

3. When do I want to go?

_____

_____

_____

_____

_____

_____

_____

_____

_____

_____

_____

_____

_____

_____

_____

_____

_____

_____

_____

_____

_____

_____

CHAPTER 6

Did you know it's estimated that eighty percent of Americans live paycheck to paycheck? Eighty percent. This is devastating, absolutely heartbreaking for me to hear. Living paycheck to paycheck leaves little room for paying down debts, living out dreams, and paying for kids' activities is nearly impossible. Luxury spending—there is none.

Living paycheck to paycheck equates to wearing handcuffs. If you are in a high-paying job and still living paycheck to paycheck, it's terrifying to think you may never break out of the cuffs!

I was a part of this eighty percent of Americans living paycheck to paycheck—nothing feels worse. It's the absolute most demoralizing feeling knowing I can't buy gifts for birthday parties until Friday comes, repeatedly checking my bank account to make sure I haven't gone negative or that there's enough to buy that cute candle from Target ... Living paycheck to paycheck feels like a strait jacket restraining you and your bank account. You JUST want to breathe.

Even high paid sales reps sometimes live paycheck to paycheck. I once heard an unforgettable story about a sales manager. Each time new sales reps joined his team, he encouraged them to buy a luxury car. "You're gonna make fast cash here and you deserve a nice car," he would say to new hires. What's scary is that his intentions had little to do with the sales reps' best interests. He encouraged this so they'd experience relentless pressure to perform and make more money ... in other words, bring in more revenue for *the man*. Ugh, everything about this seems backwards.

Working a 9-to-5 and receiving biweekly paychecks is like being stuck inside a glass box, desperately hoping to receive a raise, lifting the ceiling higher and higher each year. There are years you get a raise you deserve, but most years you're left disappointed as your minuscule or absent-altogether raise leaves you feeling worthless. Like the 9-to-5, the cycle of living paycheck to paycheck is ingrained at a young age. It's a reason that many department stores offer layaway and credit cards with no cost to activate.

By now, I probably sound like some crazy conspiracy theorist; I can assure you that is far from the truth. Why? These aren't conspiracies; these are real things that happen every single day. The entire setup of the economy was not designed for *your* benefit. It was designed to ultimately benefit *the man* in the upper tier. This is why the rich keep getting richer, and the middle class continue to find themselves in an ever-shrinking glass box.

When living paycheck to paycheck, you can't follow dreams and move on to bigger things. You can't negotiate or play hardball for fear of losing your job. You sit powerless. Something that blew the lid off my glass box and me away from living paycheck to paycheck will also help you. As boss, *you* can decide how much money you will make, when to give yourself a raise, and when you're ready to splurge on things, but first, let's talk for a second about the $100K myth.

Have you found yourself wanting to make $100,000? "If I could just make $100,000 all my problems will be solved." I used to believe this. More than anything, I just wanted to make $100,000 and get that tax return back to see that beautiful number with five *fat, juicy* zeros at the end. What I'm about to tell you may actually leave you feeling slightly discouraged, but don't worry, there's good news coming. Only about twenty percent of Americans make over $100,000 per year, which means that eighty percent of jobs don't necessarily lead to that path.

If you do have this six-figure dream, consider these questions. Does my manager make $100,000 a year? Does my boss? Better yet, does the owner of the company even make that amount? If the answer to any of these three questions is no, then your pathway to making $100,000 a year is more like a $100,000 death sentence. You're wishing for something that simply will not be offered to you, most likely, for ten, fifteen, or twenty years, provided that the economy doesn't shift drastically.

Back in 2015 when I started this incredible journey towards becoming the boss, my number one goal was to make $100,000 per year. I knew that if I could reach that goal, everything would be okay—it would be breaking the status quo. Something eye-opening I'd like to share about my journey … In 2012, I was a single mom living on welfare and food stamps. My daughter, Dakotah, and I rented one bedroom from a house with many roommates. I was an alcoholic coming from an alcoholic family, and my parents were divorced. Oh, and I had NO degree. I dropped out of college; it just wasn't for me.

According to all the statistics, there is no logical reason why I would ever be able make more than an average wage. It would defy all expectations. I knew somewhere deep down that if I could make $100,000, it would be possible for so many more people, yes, including people who are far more talented, skilled, educated, and passionate than I am.

So, in 2015, I started my journey. It began as a side hustle while I also worked an 8-to-5. After leaving that job, securing clients, and working towards this dream of the $100,000 year, I hit my first $10,000 month. Whoa, whoa, whoa—$10,000 MONTH! Did you read that? Read it again. $10,000 in ONE MONTH equates to $120,000 in a year, which leaves ample room for taxes, business expenses, and a near $100,000 take-home salary.

As I looked over the number, I cried. Everything was about to change. Now, a little side note, I had no clue that over the next couple of years, I would build a business that would usher in millions per year; I would hire a team of people locally and virtually; and I would serve thousands of people along the way, helping them to hit their first $10,000 month. That first month with four juicy, fat zeros meant I had broken through the glass ceiling. It meant that life as I knew it *was changing*.

It almost became addicting, an incredible thrill. Any time I wanted to promote myself, I didn't have to wait two years plus a round of negotiations and proving to my boss I was worthy of a raise. Instead, I would provide value, secure a new client, and bam, our income would be raised by $2,000 per month.

If you find yourself waiting for permission from your boss to make $100,000 a year, you're in a losing battle. In fact, you've already lost. Your boss and your 9-to-5 have no desire to issue $100,000 paychecks. No, they're going to require you to sell your evenings, weekends, and hand over your dreams completely. The price tag of a $100,000 per year job is actually quite devastating.

I'm sure you know an attorney or doctor. They spend their lives dedicated to their careers with crippling amounts of student loans. When talking with them, you'll often see that they're exhausted. When you ask about their life, they'll say, "Ugh, work has been so busy. I'm tired," and of course they are!

The $100K myth is that it will be enough to solve all your problems, but the biggest problem is never solved. The biggest problem is that eager part of you burning to live out your dreams and have a life full of freedom … a life with work you love, not a 9-to-5 or 5-to-9 spending your weekends and evenings with your laptop and a never-ending, always demanding pile of papers on your desk.

If you are so lucky as to make $100,000 in your 9-to-5, you know the stress and pressure isn't worth it. This isn't the life your sixteen-year-old self envisioned for you. The definition of broke, in my opinion, is not just about finances. The definition of broke is a life unlived ... with dreams collecting dust and family time ignored in lieu of the $100,000 paycheck, while waiting for you on the other side is a life of fulfillment, abundance, and yeah, wealth.

If you're a part of the eighty percent who will most likely never make $100,000, you're feeling the pressure of being broke. If you are a part of the elite twenty percent making over $100,000 per year, you're probably feeling depleted, exhausted, and like so much more is meant for you, your family, vacations, and dreams.

Even *if* you hit the $100,000 salary, you are so consumed by work, it feels like you are literally waking up and living for your paycheck, and THAT, by my definition, is another kind of broke. So, no matter which way you flip the coin, working for the man will always leave you broke, and you must know, something more awaits you!

I'm sure you're starting to see why it is so important that you become *the boss* and I am honored to lead you on this journey. It's about to get real.

CHAPTER 6 QUESTIONS FOR REFLECTION

1. Am I realistically on a path that will bring me to $100,000 in the next five years?

2. Do I look forward to the existing path to $100,000?

3. How would I feel earning $100,000 sooner?

_____

_____

_____

_____

_____

_____

_____

_____

_____

_____

_____

_____

_____

_____

_____

_____

_____

_____

_____

_____

_____

_____

_____

_____

CHAPTER 7

TGIF. This acronym is very common in the world of 9-to-5ers—Thank God It's Friday. Why do so many people look forward to Friday? For goodness sakes, TGIF is on mugs, t-shirts, notebooks, and even a restaurant bears the name. But what is it about our lives that have us so excited about the weekend? As I dove in, the answer kind of surprised me.

When we work in a 9-to-5, we start to believe weekends are the time for us to enjoy our lives. We fall into a little lull Monday through Friday, a pattern that has us holding our breath, just waiting for 5 p.m. to hit on Friday. Back when I used to work for a technology company, I'll never forget a coworker saying, "I just love weekends. Weekends are the time I get to spend with my family and work on my projects. It's just like everything is right on the weekends. Ugh, I hate when Monday comes around."

This case of "I hate Mondays" isn't caused by the natural circadian rhythm. No, it's actually part of the pendulum swing that happens when we constantly look forward to Friday. Why? Why are we constantly dreading Mondays and loving Fridays so much?

In a traditional 9-to-5 setting, working Monday through Friday, you coast, almost skate, through the week. You wake up at 7 a.m., get the kids ready, get dressed for work, commute, sit in traffic, listen to the same radio shows over and over again every single day—you might even know the DJs by name. It almost feels like they're long lost friends. They're not your friends. If they were your friends, you would also look forward to connecting with them once TGIF hit.

Starting at about 3 p.m. each day at work, you start to count down the minutes until the proverbial bell rings to set you free for the evening. However, Monday, Tuesday, Wednesday, and Thursday are not the same as Friday once 5 p.m. hits. You don't get that same feeling of freedom at 5 p.m. on those days like you do on Friday. Nope, on those days, you hop into your car, listen to the same radio shows once again, become evening friends with the DJs while you sit in rush hour traffic waiting to pick up the kids, and then … you finally head home.

At this point, it's 6 p.m. and you're tired, but guess what? Responsibilities aren't done. It's time to cook dinner, pick up the house, turn over some laundry, and start to prep for the next day all over again. Maybe you drink a glass—no, a bottle—of wine and relax, only to find yourself numbing all of the possibilities because it's not Friday yet. "Ugh, I cannot wait for TGIF," you think.

You doze off on the couch listening to the droning soundtrack of your latest Netflix binge before your spouse nudges you and says, "It's time to go to bed." You oblige, though when the alarm rings at 7 a.m., you know you did not sleep long enough.

This routine repeats Monday through Friday until finally, it's 5 p.m. on Friday. Maybe it's 4 p.m. on Friday if you have one of those really cool jobs that allow you to have that flex time. Wow, what a great benefit! Maybe? When that 4 p.m. or 5 p.m. hits on Friday though, it sure feels a little different. It's not quite like the bell of recess as you remember, but instead, it is that amazing freedom knowing the weekend is yours. It doesn't belong to your boss, it doesn't belong to your email. 5 p.m. on Friday is a very special time because now you have the ability to dive into what you've been thinking about the entire week! Perhaps you've been pinning your favorite recipes, maybe looking at new decor you want to put into your house, or maybe you're like me and you enjoy Goodwill thrift shopping on the weekends when there is no rush.

I want to propose a new theory. What if TGIF is actually a dangerous phrase? TGIF means, "finally I can make an impact on my life that I've been dreaming of all week." Hold on, one second though, because if you're like me, you have *tons* of dreams. Maybe you're planning out how you will *finally* get into the best shape of your life, or maybe you're starting to think of that perfect stylish wardrobe you've always wanted. Perhaps, you have a passion project to complete, a new language to learn, or crafts to prepare for the kids.

Here's an intriguing and scary statistic. If you have been spending Monday through Friday looking forward to the weekend, you've spent approximately five of seven days dreading, which translates to about 71.428571 percent of your week. You've wasted nearly seventy-two percent of your week because you haven't been able to do those things that your heart is *screaming* for.

Maybe you want to make an impact, maybe you want to take your family to feed the homeless, maybe you want to finally organize that closet or, as unreal as it sounds, write that book. But, you only have twenty-eight percent of your week to create the impact that you'd like to have on your kids, marriage, house, and world! Wow! I don't know about you, but I don't think that twenty-eight percent is enough time to create the impact you want.

The TGIF mentality is enough to reduce you into a cycle that leaves you desiring more, always feeling like your projects aren't full, like there is something waiting for next weekend, next month, next year, or maybe in the next lifetime. What if you could reverse that percentage? What if, and this sounds unbelievable so hang with me for a second, you could actually spend closer to seventy-two percent enjoying your week, impacting the world, finishing projects, starting new projects ... actually doing the things your soul desires?

This is why I don't believe in the TGIF mentality, and instead I offer a new alternative–TGIT. Thank God It's Today. When you flip your paradigm from TGIF to TGIT, suddenly every single day gives you the ability to create an impact. Every single day you're able to determine what you want to do. When you say, "I'm the boss of my life and that means TGIT," you're going to find that something radical happens. Suddenly, your dreams get bigger. Your ideas come to life.

I'll never forget what happened when I stopped waiting. In fact, as I write this book, something magical just happened. When I chose to live in TGIT instead of TGIF, I finally took a chance towards another big dream I had, besides of course writing this book. I saw that one of my favorite TV shows in the whole entire world was hiring for extras. Instead of saying maybe next week, next month, next year, or even maybe in the next lifetime, I said, "TGIT, let's do it."

I submitted my headshot and within twenty-four hours, I got the email that I was going to be cast on my favorite show. Sure, it's only as an extra role, but know that when you go after your dreams of impacting the world every single day instead of waiting for Friday and instead of waiting for the twenty-eight percent that's left ... know that you will achieve so much more.

Now, weekends are great, and I still enjoy weekends, but there's something different about having *massive* possibility and the *ability* to transform the world, *your* world, your kids' world, and your family's world—every single day. Weekends aren't enough, and when you start to embrace the TGIT mentality of a boss, you're going to discover that your wildest dreams are *absolutely* within reach as long as you choose them *today*.

CHAPTER 7 QUESTIONS FOR REFLECTION

1. Where do my true feelings lie when it comes to Mondays?

_____

_____

_____

_____

_____

_____

_____

_____

_____

_____

_____

_____

_____

_____

_____

_____

_____

_____

_____

_____

_____

_____

_____

_____

_____

_____

2. Do I live for the weekends?

3. What would I do if TODAY I had freedom?

_____

_____

_____

_____

_____

_____

_____

_____

_____

_____

_____

_____

_____

_____

_____

_____

_____

_____

_____

_____

_____

_____

_____

_____

_____

CHAPTER 8

So, you get it, you feel it, and you *know* deep down I am right. It's time for you to become *THE BOSS*, but first, you need to escape the boss. I wish I could tell you it's as simple as leaving your job and starting to do what you love, but then I would be a liar, and if there's one thing I don't like, it's liars. I've never been a liar, and I'm not going to start today. No, first we are going to create a clear plan so that you do not feel like you're out of control. In fact, quite the opposite is true. When you're the boss, you're in control of your life.

First things first, I need you to commit mentally to escaping the boss. What does that mean? Well, I have a beautiful gift to share with you, and that is the "I'm the Boss" Manifesto. Ready for it?

I'm the Boss. Life doesn't happen to me, it happens for me.
Because I set the rules, the constraints of society do not apply.
The programming given to me is not what I accept.
The limitations of my past do not define me.
Every day is a new day, and every day I choose the future.
I'm accepting the new path for my life, one in which
I am in charge of my destiny. *I am* free to choose
how my day starts, ends, and impacts the world.
I am redefining who I am.
I'm the Boss.

Now, the mental game will be the toughest part of all of this. Don't say I didn't warn you. The reason you need to mentally prepare yourself for leaving your 9-to-5, for escaping the boss, is because it really is a mind game. You've spent your entire life under the programming of others, and now it's time for us to truly focus on reprogramming you. So, what the heck does that look like?

I want to prepare you for all that will stand in your way. The very first hurdle you need to overcome is your own mind because it will play tricks on you.

In fact, every single time you find yourself struggling with your why, your plan, or the steps you have to take, I want you to go back to the "I'm the Boss" Manifesto and read it. Read it out loud, write it down, print it out, and say it to yourself every morning when you wake up.

Committing mentally has been a huge part of my success and that means I'm ALL IN. Before I became an entrepreneur, I didn't understand that mindset was a real thing. In fact, I'm going to be honest, I was a skeptic about this whole mindset thing. I thought mindset was something just hippie dippies believed in ... you know, that it was kind of a yoga thing or something. I didn't know exactly what it meant, but it didn't seem like something I cared about or would ever really care about until the day I started to struggle in my business, and I couldn't quite figure out the problem.

Why was I not getting leads? Why was I not closing sales? It seemed like everything was going wrong in my business. I reached out to one of my friends who owns a successful agency. When I started to unload my problems on her, she asked me one simple question. "What was it that rocked your mindset?" At first, I thought she was out of her mind, but when she told me it all came down to the commitment within my mindset, I decided to give it a try.

After spending the next few weeks immersing myself in mental commitment and focusing on my mindset game, I saw a massive shift. In fact, my business that was spiraling out of control, or at least it felt that way, completely transitioned into a thriving business in just a matter of weeks—all because of mindset. Although I love the word *mindset*, I consider this more so to be *committing mentally*. In order to get a different result from the result you've always gotten, you have to do something different, and it all starts with your mind.

Time and time again, I see new entrepreneurs, people trying to become the boss, failing to prioritize mindset. Often, they don't take mentors' advice seriously: mindset and mental commitment is *everything*. Sadly, I continue to see consequences as their businesses and happiness spiral out of control.

This is one of your greatest tools—the recognition that you are in control of your mind. Yeah, it's amazing. Dr. Caroline Leaf's talk about depression and negative thoughts had a profound impact on me. She said the thoughts we dwell on ultimately determine the patterns, brainwaves, and the connections within our brains. Quite literally, what we focus on and think about creates pathways in our brains that continue creating those thoughts; so, we have to commit one hundred percent to having a focused, healthy, and positive mindset. The mental game is everything.

I control my mind a couple different ways, and no, they're not directly related to revenue or leaving my 9-to-5, or even to the marketing strategies it takes to become the boss. In fact, it all starts with believing in myself, and I want you to do the same thing. One of the best ways to control your thoughts is with morning affirmations, regardless of when you wake up. Choose your thoughts based on your desires.

Now, I've heard people poo-poo affirmations, but let me tell you, the reason affirmations work is because you are literally creating the possibilities in your brain. You are programming your mind for success. Just like athletes program their minds and visualize that game-winning shot, you have to program your mind every single day. You have to visualize yourself becoming the boss.

What does that look like for you? Let's take a moment and truly envision your game-winning shot. What does it look like to be the boss of your life? What does it feel like to turn in your notice to your boss and no longer be imprisoned by your 9-to-5? What does it look like to freely live out your dreams? Which dreams come first?

You must commit to *being* the person you need to be in order to create those dreams. Before we dive into the tactical strategies and methods we'll use to set you up for success, I need to prepare you for one more thing. People who love you and care about you may *not* be ready for the idea that you're going to pursue something different. In fact, most people will think you are crazy, but know, I am on your side.

Your dreams, your hopes, even your day-to-day plans or goals are not meant to be shared with everyone because not everyone understands the processes you will implement, the growth you'll experience, and person you need to become in order to be the boss of your life. If that sounds intimidating, think of it as a prized possession. Your dreams and your vision both need to be protected, and anyone who does not give you positivity, affirmation, and encouragement cannot be a part of your mental game.

Commitment means surrounding yourself with others who are on the same wavelength, can support you, have been there, and know what you need in order to make this a reality. A great way to do that is by joining the "I'm the Boss Challenge" where you'll be surrounded by other people who have the same goals as you, or at least some of the same goals since no two people are exactly alike.

You will come up against challenges and will have one of two choices. You can keep going on the path you've been on and know that nothing is going to change, or you can embrace the challenges that will certainly come up as you embark on this journey. Come up with several words you can identify with. Maybe they're your own affirmations. "I am

strong." "I am full of grit." "I am tenacious." "I am passion-
ate." "I am committed." "I am a Pitbull." Choose whatever
it is that makes you feel alive and ready to act. Create affirmations that remind you of the commitment that you have
mentally made to escape the 9-to-5.

When the going gets tough, I remember why I'm doing
all of this. I journal exactly what my dreams and visualiza-
tions hold so I can look back and say *this* is what I'm working
towards. *This* is what makes the sacrifice worth it.

In the first couple of years of my business, I worked a *lot*.
I certainly don't recommend this for everyone, but I worked
eighty to one hundred hours every week because I knew I
wanted to build something massive. Not everyone will or
should take this path. Not everyone wants a multi-million
dollar business or even a billion dollar business. Not everyone
wants fame and recognition and the responsibility to speak
and travel the world.

In 2018 alone, I boarded approximately fifty flights.
(I don't have an exact number because just the thought of
it makes me dizzy.) In order to accomplish all I want to
accomplish, it requires a lot of hard work (and that means an
insane work ethic). It means being a lion, being confident,
and standing strong in the face of adversity, because trust me,
it will happen.

You will also experience stepping outside your comfort
zone. Stepping outside of your comfort zone means you will
feel very uncomfortable at times. You will be challenged. You
will question everything you know—who you are and what
you're made of, but the journey and what you discover along
the way makes it absolutely worth it.

Imagine yourself fully alive as the boss of your life and
feel the strength rising up inside of you. Think about how
you will respond when you hear someone say, "I don't know."
Appreciate that little voice that now reassures you, saying,
"But I know! I know who I am, and I know what I'm called

to do!" Embrace the rebel you're made of because if you're reading this book, you're not a doormat. You are a natural born leader. You are a boss, even if it's just the boss of yourself. A part of you wants to prove the doubters wrong. A part of you wants to doubt "doubt" itself. If this is all speaking to you, you're in the right place.

You're the Boss.

CHAPTER 8 QUESTIONS FOR REFLECTION

1. Who do I admire in terms of their tenacity and grit?

_____

_____

_____

_____

_____

_____

_____

_____

_____

_____

_____

_____

_____

_____

_____

_____

_____

_____

_____

_____

_____

_____

_____

_____

_____

_____

2. What am I willing to do in order to become the boss of
   my life?

_____

_____

_____

_____

_____

_____

_____

_____

_____

_____

_____

_____

_____

_____

_____

_____

_____

_____

_____

_____

_____

_____

_____

3. Am I ready to stop at NOTHING to become the boss?

_____
_____
_____
_____
_____
_____
_____
_____
_____
_____
_____
_____
_____
_____
_____
_____
_____
_____
_____
_____
_____
_____
_____
_____
_____
_____

What if you could quickly
build a business learning
the same methods that have
taken me years to master?

Discover what true freedom
feels like...

www.joinsmu.com

CPSIA information can be obtained
at www.ICGtesting.com
Printed in the USA
BVHW041055170620
581539BV00007B/806

9 781640 859029